Light Light

Light Light

JULIE JOOSTEN

BookThug

2013

FIRST EDITION

Copyright © Julie Joosten, 2013

Cover image: A cyanotype of the fern *Asplenium chinensis*, from *Cyanotypes of British and Foreign Ferns* (1853), by Anna Atkins. Interior images: Page 11: A cyanotype of *Laminaria phyllitis*, Page 47: A cyanotype of *Delesseria hypoglossum*; Page 67: A cyanotype of *Gigartina Griffithsiae*. All from *Photographs of British algae: cyanotype impressions* (1843-1853) by Anna Atkins.

The production of this book was made possible through the generous assistance of The Canada Council for the Arts and The Ontario Arts Council.

Canada Council **Conseil des Arts**
for the Arts **du Canada**

ONTARIO ARTS COUNCIL
CONSEIL DES ARTS DE L'ONTARIO
50 YEARS OF ONTARIO GOVERNMENT SUPPORT OF THE ARTS
50 ANS DE SOUTIEN DU GOUVERNEMENT DE L'ONTARIO AUX ARTS

LIBRARY AND ARCHIVES CANADA CATALOGUING IN PUBLICATION

Joosten, Julie, 1980-, author
      Light light / Julie Joosten.

Poems.
Issued in print and electronic formats.
ISBN 978-1-927040-83-6 (pbk.). – ISBN 978-1-927040-95-9 (epub). –
ISBN 978-1-77166-011-2 (pdf). – ISBN 978-1-77166-021-1 (mobi)

      I. Title.

PS8619.O68L53 2013   C811'.6   C2013-904329-2
                                         C2013-904330-6

for my family

Contents

And then like this: that a feeling begins,
because flower petals touch flower petals?
And this: that one opens like a lid,
and under it lie only eyelids,
all closed, as if they, sleeping tenfold,
had to damp an inner power of sight.
And this above all: that through these petals
light must pass.

– RAINER MARIE RILKE

Wind

The wind is a tongue to watch or touch.

In it, a post with a hole bored by a beetle and three holes fissured by drying. A violet trumpet vine extends a tendril, gentles into a hole, withdraws.

Were the vine an animal, its motion would be instinct, the tendril's spire turning through ellipses of thought.

Proof anticipates direction. It is noon repeatedly, sky repeatedly. It is wind repeatedly, the moon rising or setting in declensions of light.

To infer an existence.

Thinking, by analogy, of fossilized plants, of how little of life is alive in the world.

How in a little hole a tendril may keep its point for twenty hours perhaps, or thirty-six, then withdraw.

We extend to accompany the plant.

We sway in the hatchery, learn synchrony from the silkworm.

Tenses forget to pass or pass imperceptibly: silk moth above a mulberry tree, caterpillar on a leaf, white pupa bending moonlight.

How fruit drops in a concordance.

A wasp crawls from a caterpillar cocoon.

Your eyes bend the light in your hands.

A surface to trace with the eye, to trace the eye with.

To grow by looking. Little peering efforts unexpectedly given.

Shadow of a hovering kestrel. Purple-starred hepatica. A rough sea.

I lick fog, taste evening. Invite forgetfulness as a way to perceive you, to let hepatica become a sensation without thought: a purple sea spreading in sunlight.

Here I feel myself there – the other side of the sea.

A kestrel's shadow hovers on the sea's surface.

Quanta of light move in waves over the sea, move the sea to the horizon.

Purple is a horizon extending the sky.

It seems not an earth-sky.

To think of attention as moving without trying to be moved to shadow, hepatica, sea, to purple or sky.

Rain falls on the sea and forms a night field of circles glittering idly in moonlight then dissolves into sea surface.

To give attention to what does not exist.

Here, there.

Ghost Species

Henry David Thoreau would describe the seasons, listing

the flowering times of wildflowers around Concord Massachusetts
(1851-1858).

It continues today: the data, the occasional field, the wildflowers,
declining.

Temperatures warm, and surviving species flower now about seven
days earlier than they did in the mid-nineteenth century.

Species sensitive to temperature have been best able to survive,
best able, perhaps, to maintain synchronicity with other plants,
pollinators, and predators.

The ghostliness of seasonal change, an orchid coming to flower
overnight.

Species unresponsive to temperature have decreased in abundance.

Lapsing species become, for a moment, ghosts,

place-faithful, they persist after the ending of their environments.

Exiled in stillness, then, in a moment, slipping out of life.

Wind Scene

Zhuangzi (circa 370-286 BCE) writes of an Old Woman with skin "as bright as snow." Asked how she achieves her childlike complexion, the Old Woman answers, "By clarifying and decanting day after day, little by little I perceive the whole world, things, and even life itself as external to me. They no longer burden my vitality. I live then in the transparency of morning."

To keep by purifying, life eludes its own grasp, is fed.

Breath by breath, thought by thought, an incremental withdrawal leaves not nothing but an openness that assumes the gradualness of dimension.

There, vitality comes and goes.

The Old Woman takes shape around, is the shape of, a gentle wind passing through the pear tree.

Wardian Case / Terrarium

As Thoreau was cataloguing flowers

a British ship came riding
from Shanghai, was a trough toward Calcutta (1851)
the ship's direction making crests from desire
carrying thousands of stolen seedlings.

An empire on the principle of the terrarium: in an enclosed
case, plants grow
                        fed only by light, watered only by
moisture condensed from the heat of the day and
returned to the soil at night.

The tea seedlings were packed in sixteen Wardian cases,
boxes with glass sides and tops (later in the century
Darwin would write, "light [acts] on the tissue of plants almost
in the same manner as it does on the nervous system
of an animal").

It was an accident, Ward's discovery.

To watch the chrysalis of a sphinx moth metamorphose,
Ward covered it with a glass jar (the hills of Darjeeling
turned, too, turned green, then tended and pruned, turned empire)

and beneath the chrysalis, common grass and a rare fern sprouted.

Rain

A wave propagates disturbance in a quiescent state

As if quiescence must always dissolve into action, as if stillness wavers to remain still

Then wavers to light or sound

My breathing or the beating of my heart disturbs the movement of tall grass in the wind

A bee buzzes, rhythmizing perception in waves

I anticipate gravity as a density of light, light as an atmosphere of dissolve

To see a landscape as it is when no one is there

Cells loosen and energy rises in stem and sepal, draws out an arc of thought, opalescent

Sense adapts thought's tangent as an arc between the sun and the horizon

As a change in timbre not yet voice or horn

Once we know we are nothing

Not a cloud in the sky

Our effort is to become nothing

When you think of me I root in the absence of a place

A joy so perfect it cannot be felt, the soul left no corner, filled with its object, for feeling

We encompass ourselves by leaving

Ride out of the city

A translucent building burns on a plain

Its flames trace the wind's inflection

To be only an intermediary you say

Between storm cloud and calmed fire

Between electricity and a watered root

To love without interpretation

And rain intransitively

The mereness of rain, its simple happening

The sky takes over between us

We love distance as a weather of shapes: road, plain, border, ocean,
thought

Desire extends outward in a field of radials forming not your hand
but the motion of its tiny bones

The pleasure that you exist

You a source of thought, not its object

It rains

You reach for an umbrella and open it

Wind Scene

Simone Weil writes of her time working in a vineyard, "I recited Our Father in Greek every day before work, and I repeated it very often in the Vineyard. Since that time I have made a practice of saying it through once each morning with absolute attention [. . . .] At times the very first words tear my thoughts from my body and transport it to a place outside space where there is neither perspective nor point of view."

Perspective is torn in an attention, I think, specific to morning and its relinquishments, to a calm that precedes individuation. .

Morning, thought, and body come to exist outside space.

Diffuse and transforming, attention emanates indefinitely here, a vital form of being, the morning's transparency.

It clears a way; wind pulses through the vineyard, breathes between branches and leaves, turns them into breath.

If light stabilizing / If to receive a bee

I've read that the art of the solitary hunter is empathy: taking time
the hunter invites the hunted's subtlety

                                into her own.

A bee orchid appears
to have a bee or wasp resting
on it and its petals
give off the scent of female bees.

These contrivances lure male bees to the orchid in a deception so
complete a bee will devote itself briefly, entirely to the orchid,
pseudo-mating with it.

In this excitement the bee is covered in pollen and pollinates the
orchids it later visits.

Flowers appear as bees
entice them
are violated by them

In this story the bee orchid is not empathic but offers a lesson in
subtlety.

Enchanted by subtleness Maria Sibylla Merian (1647-1717) studied
and drew the metamorphoses of insects

processes whose
minute alterations
are so
gradual
as
to be
almost
imperceptible.

Of looking in curiosity cabinets, Merian:

"I found these
and numerous other
insects but such
that their origins
and reproduction
were lacking,
that means,
how
    they
        changed

        from caterpillars
        into pupae
        and
        so forth.

All this inspired me
to take a long . . .
and 'costly,' expensive
journey and
go to Surinam

[...]
in order to continue
my observations
there."

Merian after whom eventually six species of plants nine butterflies
and two beetles were named

Merian who voyaged solely for science.

Voyaging [as] a form
of hunting
hunting a form
of worship

collecting caterpillars
in the cool of
morning
preparing them
in the evening
with the sun
setting

overseeing
the uprooting of
plants in the forest
and along rivers and
their replanting
in a garden

watching as plants
grow bloom blow
and following the insects
that visit them
in these unfoldings

attending to the silent
transformations
of caterpillars
camouflaged
on stems and leaves.

Prayer not
as petition
but as attention,
an unexpected
grace:

thought (also
called love) becomes
an indirect light stabilizing
perception in a self
ceasing to be

to attend to the existence
of caterpillars
of orchids.

Qualities of light:
slant, reflectivity,
colour, illumination

empathy
without seizure

light's ability to
receive a bee
an ocean a
ship while
retracting itself
from view.

Eighteenth- and nineteenth-century botanical illustrations arrived
in Amsterdam Paris London Madrid in crates by maritime post

the figure of an orchid or a peacock flower

islanded   on   a
          white   page   flowering
in   static   lushness

having dissolved geography
                    local knowledge
                    use and
                    name

as if in saltwater

crossing the sea.

You don't think
of form
by the sea.

(Agnotology: the study of culturally produced ignorances.
Agnotology extends the questions 'what and how we know' to
include 'what we do not know,' and 'how we do not know it.')

I don't know
the Arawak
or the Carib
name for
peacock flower.

No one does anymore.

Merian relied on Amerindian and African slaves to help her find choice specimens and to protect her in her travels.

She called them *myne Slaven*.

They, nameless, cut
openings for her
to pass through
dense forests paddled
her along rivers dug
up roots planted
and helped tend her
garden

gave maggots
caterpillars fireflies
gave shells and
peacock flowers.

The elegant peacock flower,
Flos pavonis Merian called it,

is inflorescent
                        which sounds
like a quality
                        of light
                        or lightness

but designates
a cluster of flowers
arranged on a stem.

The peacock flower has 20-30 flaming red and yellow flowers.
Merian's depiction (plate 45 of her *Metamorphosis Insectorum
Surinamensium* (1705)) includes the plant's

leaves burnished seeds and glowing
flowers

along with three stages
of the tobacco hornworm
moth: light sea-green
caterpillar red pupa and
a large moth with a snaking
proboscis

gathering nectar
from a flower.

Merian wrote, "The Indians, who are not

treated well
by their Dutch masters,

use the seeds [of the peacock flower] to abort

their children,
                        so that their children
                        will not become
slaves / like they
are.

The black slaves
                        from Guinea and Angola
                        have demanded to be

well treated, threatening
to refuse to

have
children
[...]

They told me this themselves."

Told me this themselves
often preferring to say
nothing

secrecy another form
of resistance

lying – from this "worm"
a "handsome grasshopper" –
another.

(Following
this description,
Merian drew
a beetle larva
two praying mantises
and an egg cocoon
on a lush nipple fruit
full of deep greens and
shining yellows
(plate 27)

documenting what
the slaves told her)

To trace a trade route
by which something did
not happen:

knowledge
of the abortive
powers of
the peacock
flower did
not travel
with the plant

to European gardens and curiosity cabinets and was never noted in
medical encyclopedias or herbalist manuals.

It is difficult to look at the sun

Quiet on the floor of a house you can enter
if you encounter nothing

slave women, peacock flowers, mothers

of unhappening.

Once Sun

It began a field, grew valley. Light tipped grass scatters from pollen. Tree atoms gather in splints, divide to aster and cress.

Became a room of weather.

The sun coppers the ground. Its angles bring several seasons at once.

The accident of petals quarrying a winter field.

In a valley of wild hive, orange blossom, and honey the sun is silent. Is carried on the backs of horses.

Ferried against the wind.

By sympathy or suggestion I remember what I am. Walking beside a river humming with the dark.

The yellow tip of the tree shakes in the wind. The eye sees what the ear misses behind glass.

A field of light amplified stretches the eye's limit. Gives the limit of the eye as a horizon of mountain and sky that may be the shadow of clouds or may be a mountain.

I think you can climb them. A cairn, a fragment, a beam.

The eye makes.

A woman piles wood under a red barn door held up by four stakes in the centre of a field.

I can't turn away. Even when the edges of the wood blur. I stop seeing because I feel in my mind as if I'm touching it.

Or because of the pleasure of the stuckness of my eyes. Held by nothing and not wanting to blink or turn away.

The mind like that.

The green of the field felt so unforgettable winter could never again exist.

I'd have said in the absence of colour there thought was. The hills bringing the mind not to itself but to the idea of green. To the feeling of sunlight as expectation. The future opened from a circle of snow.

Stone, maple, daffodil, tadpole, skein.

When the valley came to be a valley I was watching winter grasses brown against the sky then green then suddenly in a startling smallness bud to pink. But it wasn't as peaceful as that. Mud thickened the ground, made it grabby.

It gripped a finch, spit up feathers to write with, took an oak, four kittens, a thunderstorm, and a pair of woolen gloves. Grabbed a man and a woman whole, left imprints like swollen snow angels.

In place of winter a field emerged, carving beauty's furrows, entrenching muck-splattered beauty into the valley.

I was to guard the valley, name it, speak to it by name.

Speak constatives   The wind blows   It rains   The night hums
Then speak to constellate   an uncertain heaven   winding rain of
weathershroud   certainly light hollows the reign of day   eclipses the
moon   An unexpected face raises the sky   trilling light   returns in
the old way   stone bearing water   Comte said the brain   is a device
in which the dead act   on the living   occipital cathedral   Open the
sky   Consent to field to frame of light

The light shapes the quiet as morning.
The light settles a shawl over the frozen ground.
To light out.
One hill at a time, the light moves in strides, covering.
The light blocked by birds, a shadow-pattern of flight on the road the roof the river.
Light-splintered.
The light enskyed.
The light gentles the daffodil upward.
The light uninterpretable.
The light losing our words.
A filament of light.
The light shakes the leaves.
Strike a light.
The light with night coming on.
The light begging pardon.
The light burning in my hand.
Eyeless light.
Light laments.
The lighthouse revolving.
The refrangible light of the sun.
The optic nerve the light excites.
Vibrating light.
Light-embroidered.
The warmth of light on your skin.
Daybreak.

(The valley carries
cemeteries in its mouth, grounds sound
to seed and buries it –
there is a world and the world inside it –)

This the haunting dissension, an elaboration of the blind field, its quickening cast out from the eye, shivering into gestures of birds, the ground mottled with flight. The clothes on the bank tell the river of others. Side-saddled skirts hang the horse's back. The heartbeat of the horse. To touch that stake of pulse, marrow light held in the hand, whalebone stays hovering the skirt. Ghost's corsetry. The way, falling at a certain angle, rain severs the eye.

If weather   dresses wind whiter

if drowning   cliff and valley foundering

night foaling morning   if storm fronting

anvil cloud tumbling   horse striking

darkness deeper piling   if flint

if fist   if gibbet   if bide   if sky

From the half-lit lip of sky I tip away
so gently I can speak only in place of
have felt my mouth rash with
riding, driving, pulling chariot, buggy, cart,
I plummet, I rifle, I debt unsung –

I woke in almost night. Conscious of nothing else. Nothing but sky and stars and a few leaves. And then the delight of them.

The sky and stars and leaves the feeling of nothing conscious. Nothing the feeling of delight. I woke to delight under an almost dark sky.

Entirely now, I could remember nothing. The present was an expanse with stars in a darkening with leaves in the air.

Then being born again as the lightness of stars and leaves. I had no notion of myself as a person. I had a notion of nothing, the delightful sky I woke to.

I didn't know who I was or where I was. The wonderful calm of forgetfulness. Each time I recall it there is nothing to compare it to. Remembering forgetting as an incomparable delight and calm.

(waking into which
room with dogwood
brushing the window
pane or bird's egg
blue walls or

which door let me
light in you, scant
handiwork, the way

a pigeon flying
in stone
corridors sounds
like the sea)

When the wind blows, the house shakes.

The weather today is nettle and cloudwrath.

When you enter the room, I blush. I can't escape myself, but once on the stairs, you walked down ahead of me, my soul, I swear, walked yours with you.

Lightning seed inhabitation, lightening second, I blushed to realize that this can happen, the soul can travel between bodies.

And you turned and smiled.

And this is love, I thought, leaving the body and returning to it, life thriving like that.

Why can't I say so.

The marrow bareness of it, feeling myself stairs below myself, nested for a moment.

(the feeling of being
as it might tremble
in an animal

little is such mooring
you might tend a quiver
between you and
the dog on your lap

little, you say
as you wake
pulling yourself
through that tremble
together again)

When birdsong quickens the air, notes veering to gust or squall, the atmosphere becomes tempestuous succor or defense.

Particles of sound turn to snow.

I feel your voice on my skin, the air thick and white, the snow murmuring in the sky, sunlight quiet in the trees.

When the night is cold and clear and the ground lets go its heat, fog hums in the valley.

Moon offers a vibrating expanse.

Night-texture is cumulus, moving an ocean from one hand to the other.

Moving between the plane of the body's action and the plane of the mind's thought, life ventures out on a thread of song.

Invents a new plane, spinning record of the gramophone.

A voice carried in the wind. Or a horn buckling the sky.

Many birds open themselves to the songs of other species if they hear them during a critical period. They sing alien songs.

From across the room, I hear your hand placing the needle into a spiral of song. The spiral opens sound into space.

Your hand assures me of hands. A transparent voice, bodiless as air, opens our lungs.

Objects and gestures extend to become signs and signs become an alphabet. We learned words from wildflowers declining in the field, anemones and buttercups, asters, campanulas, goldenrods, pussytoes and thistles, bedstraws and bluets, bladderworts, dogwoods, lilies, louseworts and Indian paintbrushes, mints, orchids, primroses, roses, saxifrages, Indian pipes, St. John's worts, and violets. We read flowering times from a countryside map sown by hand. The then and now the never to come will have been flowering in the species slipped from the sun. The fax was broken, the internet too abstract. We sent messages by radio, telegraph, pigeon, balloon. *The flowers stop the flowers stop the advancing march of spring flowering stop* We couldn't forget the careful catalogues from the 1850s or the disappearance of several fields of sight.

The glasshouse burned to the ground. Strange tameness of night flocks, of electricity. I thought I'd have been myself stricken, would countenance grief with stillness. Right hand, son of my, I coughed through ash. No more, I lost a beautiful estate. A wave, hush, hush, washes between us, falls, and leaves nothing. You came in joy, once sun, threaded sky and sea, you co-extended my idea, withdrew from sight. From too much hope of thee. I could not grieve. And so grieved grief. How very much we die, so many several times. The sun-estate I couldn't touch, not even as it burned. I didn't want to keep it, but to feel its glass, the field brightening the sky from the ground up. There was an owl, a thistle moon. And I could hear torrents. The lowing cow took the whole night to die, to be a horn unbuttoning the sky, then a horse crowding the gate. I didn't know how to be. If not make the field an innavigable ocean, if not stand where it might dampen fire.

If you came from the field, born like grass, and the hutch of sun that held cloud and no rain, that weighted rain in the antechamber of your mountain, a small hill bearing weather with the reserve of a regiment newly outfitted but seasoned nonetheless by early scraps in first, uncertain days, if in the morning you woke in the field and then hammered a bird skull, white as surrender, to a nearby birch, giving vision texture, the bone whites extending into the plane of sight and straight through that to the hold of touch, if it began with perception and will end with perception, and you hold me close when it breaks, close enough to hear the cracking but not to feel its vibration, when you, eating birch bark, carrying me on your back, sweetish, licking the trees, melt snow in your mouth and feed me, you may see a horse among rocks, see it unsaddle the field.

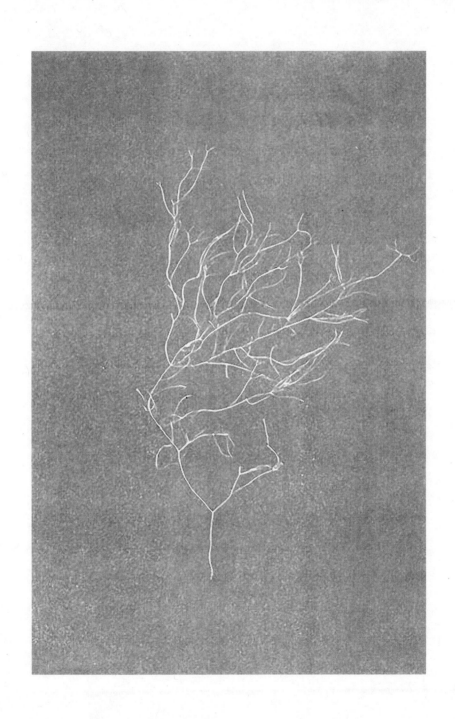

The Cause Closest to the Body

The voice is not an invisible thing as lungs under the skin.

The heart can be held in the hand.

If I tremble into H.

Not my hand, this hand, only hand.

Heart in hand.

Here, take this, gift of an H, take it as given.

If the heart in the hand sings like a thrush.

If learning by heart what is held in the hand.

The thrush in the hand beats like a heart.

The human is given, the hand sings.

Two notes at once.

One rising, one falling.

Your first cut is a deep Y through the arcing chest.

Your second, a V through the slender neck.

Lungs, bronchi, larynx, mouth, nose –

Yours is the hand singing the knife, singing buzz, saw, buzz, the voice unfolding the skin, saying hush now hush.

Rocking the head in the boat of your hand.

Rocking the brain from the home of the skull.

Tempting the song subtler: *ay ay ay.*

Yours is the heart I know by hand.

It says, what is a voice, touch me.

Wind Scene

Keats writes in a letter to his friend Reynolds: "Let us open our leaves like a flower and be passive and receptive [. . .] I was led in these thoughts, dear Reynolds, by the beauty of the morning operating on a sense of Idleness – I have not read any Books – the Morning said I was right – I had no idea but of the Morning."

The beauty of the morning, its transparency, becomes thought.

Dissolves identity in reception, in feeling an idea of the Morning.

This feeling belongs to no one in particular; "a sense of Idleness" is as much the beauty of the Morning's as Keats's own, Keats who becomes for the morning the Morning.

How astonishingly abstract the body and soul are by comparison.

The Morning sends out a small wind, carries a bee along, and brushes pollen from the combs of the bee's legs.

Pollen lingers in a swirl and surfaces on the open cup of a poppy.

Sky Georgic

Purple morning glories climb a fence among beans

We're at home here

Worry a latitude becomes a lassitude of thought

We plant bulbs for a fragile hypothesis of spring

Then take the feeling of being at home into exile

Cascarilla on a windswept tundra, the sun in every direction

We follow the weather

Are passionately impersonal

Nimbus clouds have crossed, are crossing, will cross, will have
crossed

The ocean again

It rains. It snows. It dissolves. It evaporates.

It, electric, extends invisibility

The mind is a mood of electricity, warmth, water, and wind

We trace an economy of light, mobilize distance

The sky, as we watch it drift and come apart, gives no sense of itself before

We follow the trade routes

Investigate the flora and fauna of the viceroyalty, tarry along the imperial frontier, chart coastlines

We draft maps, particularly of lesser known and contested areas, and conduct astronomical observations and measurements

We read about the politics

Attending to angles of dissidence that extend beyond the
measurement of cloud ceilings and temperatures

We paint atomic cartographies using pigments formed from achiote,
dahlia, saffron, indigo, and lichens

At a great remove becomes a way of tracing atmospheric exchange
between continents and oceans, between evolution and fallout

The aerial movement of geopolitical forces reflects the distance
clouds cover

Past sea blooms and oozy woods

Persistent sky-watching

The whale shape a cloud makes, the lion beside it

By what laws does a body dissolve, leaving behind nothing but a
negative,

a radiation shadow?

A little wind, an unseasonable cloud crosses a field

The future suggests a precipitous accumulation of the present

We point here and there, saying cirrostratus cirrus cirrocumulus
altostratus

altocumulus cumulonimbus stratocumulus stratus

nimbostratus cumulus

fog

Acquire a knowledge of blue, its refusals

There is no fair proportion of the sky

To broadcast rejects the row, sows grain over an entire field

How to make a field of standing corn

How to make it glad

Storm Front Then

If there's a river to music and a current to whiter than birch.

If A is to arc or amnesty.

If to light is to cross slight snow (stone still and wan in sunlight).

If flight to bird's wing is sunlight.

If you find yourself in a room with a piano, and you find you know how to play, the remains of the room opening onto a field, if you find music and a soldier who cannot remember his name to turn the pages, perhaps begin playing, notes shuddering into wasps' wings, into black ink of the iris, a winter shore you can't help remembering, low notes of laughter, candlelight.

(If room, hands.

If hands, piano, perhaps.

One or perhaps two.

Skies perhaps.)

If you find yourself breathless in an empty room and unhinge the ceiling with your hands to open out a full moon that returns in the future as a violet, dwindling away.

There is talk of horsepower because you were born in a buggy, but you shuttle through space on the thrust of engines.

They purr, throttle, demure before the horse that pulled the piano from your parents' house to this one.

The bullet that struck you, cavalry, contained traces of arsenic.

Arsenic preserves wood, but it is best not to burn wood preserved by it.

If from the ground walls and from the sky ceiling, if piano from trees, and the horizon from the glance of a bayonet into the sun.

If we forget the keys, the lock, the frame, have forgotten the door altogether.

Rifle a pear, call up russet and the juice of plums, know a plum is for eating.

The mouth, the tongue, the teeth.

Recall the dangers of ice, of marching through trees.

The angle of light as we step and hold a moment – comprehension as time not space, doubt as time, too – that angle of light, as we, the morning quiet keening into dawn, feel our hearts about to burst, settles soft upon the day.

We are quiet in the trees.

Walk silence out of the ground.

If, playing the piano, your left hand reaches over your right, you won't notice my distortion in a black pond.

Your playing travels through water. The current moves in ten directions at once.

The way snow falls.

I can hear your voice as you play, neither speaking nor singing. Not humming either.

A threshold.

Dust clouds scatter blue light. A red moon rises.

Red, the colour of the dark.

Tenderness is a kind
of touch. When you touch me
and I'm looking at the orchid
tenderness moves between us

                  as an electrical current.

The orchid may respond
with infinitesimally small
movements as it moves

in response to light, gravity, heat, moisture, electromagnetic
fields, electrical
        flux, and wind.

As it responds to touch.

When you look at me as I'm watering the orchid
tenderness moves between us
            as water moves
        through the roots
              of the plant

the roots determining which signals to honour.

Perception and action
occur
so gradually

that they are often too subtle
            to be
noticed
            by our senses,
accustomed to such different
            speeds.

To follow their motion, Darwin attached small instruments
                        to plants, tracing
                their intricate
                        movements
                on glass.

Darwin, *The Power of Movement in Plants:*

"It is hardly an exaggeration
to say that the tip of the radicle
thus endowed, and having the power
of directing the movements
of the adjoining parts, acts
like the brain

of one of the lower
animals; the brain being
seated within the anterior end
of the body, receiving
impressions from the sense-organs,
and directing the several
movements" (1880).

Plant neurobiology hypothesizes that the integration and
transmission of information at the plant level involves
neuron-like processes,

                            such as action potentials, long-distance
electrical signalling

            (when I learned of the body's meridians
            how, as electricity moves through them, the more-than-body –
            the soul body or energy body – may become perceptible
                        I thought of ivy
                        its electrical
                                    memory and movement)

and vesicle-mediated transport
                            of neurotransmitter-like auxin.

Light-foraging.

Along a Lambent Contour

The image a pale blue
if the leaf is semi-transparent

white if it is opaque.

Cyanotype was photography before the camera.

Anna Atkins (1799-1871), considered the first female photographer, was the first person to illuminate a book entirely with photographs.

Photographs of British Algae: Cyanotype Impressions is an encyclopedic work cataloguing algae found off the coasts of Britain.

The algae, floating on an oceanic page, seem to be a picture of livingness

then branches of lightning, a fleeting galaxy, evaporating smoke.

The light-blocking
shape of the plant cuts
infinitesimally into
the chemically prepared
surface

rather than resting
        like pollen
                on it

(anticipating Darwin's glass, his delicate
            drawing
devices).

Photosensitive
paper responds to light

where the object is not
so the shape is a shadow

the light drawing a negative
the photograph's stillness

registering light's motion
a concern with life

its withdrawal, a shadow
specimen on a blue page

is a part of our experience
that takes place elsewhere

in the time frame of a plant
moving infinitesimally

in space.

In reflexive light, a perception of the world is given rather than the world itself.

It passes into the mind with the ease of a filmy object of memory.

Or seems to pass from the mind to the paper.

In blue there was always that tremor, that airy touch.

As if light materializes
in the making
and imagining, too,
becomes perceptible
an image of lapsing
the plant's becoming
and having become
immaterial

the appearance of
latency in the present
particular, perhaps,
to the photograph

to a time
keeping with
plants.

Wind Scene

Agnes Martin writes of her gridwork painting "Morning" (1965):
"To myself and to some others there is a lot of difference between one
work and another – difference in meaning. There are many different
happinesses and blisses. 'Morning' a wonderful dawn, soft, and fresh
– before daily care takes hold. It is about how we feel."

About feeling that extends along a line, a plane, a field of attention.

The gridwork stretches beyond the opacity of daily care, allowing
happiness and bliss to be perceived as morning, its transparency.

It moves in the realm of the physical and concrete without being
encumbered by their limits.

Intersecting winds, "sublimely unemphatic," let life pass by.

Contentment in that passing.

Light Fragments

the light with night coming on

Night grows thunder in this light of strange increase.

We feel attention as duration, sense a pulse barely perceptible.
Between light whitening the sky and dissolving. Then between dark
and thunder.

It pulses again.

Attention becomes distance, lingers on a field of light receding
quietly as snow.

Diminishing where once it grew.

the light enskyed

To ease increase, you free yourself from thought.

Become self-forgetful.

Lingering, your hand touches the inclination of quiet.

The sun is silent.

You feel it not as warmth but as a light sense of being.

As if living had a fragile surface to be touched, to be touched by.

And perception were a skin.

light-embroidered

Sometimes I have the fragment of a memory that's yours.

On a kitchen table a flower stem extends perfectly along an angle of light until the light and stem disappear in a vase.

I believe for a second that light begins in a vase on a table in a kitchen.

And unfolds as day.

the light shapes the quiet as morning

You say there is no hearer but only hearing and I agree, being nothing at this moment but opening into sound. A wave washes between us. You touch it, and I listen to your fingers. Touching the wave sounds like the sea. A transparent thought dissolves and gathers a deep night color. Light plays across its surfaces. The wave rises, the sky follows. We sense day emerging as a triangle. Its constitution as a thought between us. Light brushes up against the hush-hushing of the blueing wave and warms it.

light laments

Come night, leave light light.
The very trees are pressed, their branches
green with love. If trees are mourners,
no marvel I.

Blind light, drown the stars in flood.
All sight looks lost. Bury kindled fires,
love-burnt star, shut off.

Once day takes off, I can't grieve
my thought. Grief welcomes night,
all hope and yet delay.

a filament of light

An ecology of intensities. Chlorophyll confers the faculty of feeding on light. Hair-breadths of light dangle deliciously, open resilient margins of attention. The miniscule trembles. Absorption and loss are labour. This is a tacit intimacy, an energetic discordance of vibrating cells. The sun hangs before colour, energy tied up.

the light burning in my hand

This takes nothing away.

The apricot still on the cart, trembling in the sun.

Pollen spun, it buds to branch.

If you cut out my abdomen like the bee's, and if I drink with the tongue.

Mouth theft, throat theft.

Nectar falls from the body and tapers as gentle as – tapers as quiet as –

Tapers into cups of parcelled light, the bee beside itself, dripping.

Neither mandible nor rib neither sternum nor wrist neither wing nor –

blind spot

embryo light

The light increased, unfolding an ocean of mist, covering everything. I floated on a beam, the mind covered over too. Then the shape of near trees dimly seen and dilated. The shapes of the mist, slowly moving along, passing over sheep with more of life almost than the quiet animals.

to light out

Thoreau noted grief has that bronze colour of the moon eclipsed.

the refrangible light of the sun

The fragile balance between external chance and internal openness

or, the soul's transitivity

the light losing our words

Once in a field of abandoned hives.

Once with my eyes I, ghostly, felt a river dry to clay, lay quiet beneath
a blank sky.

Once there was a field, a river, there were mountains, I saw
reflections like phantoms, a surface of forgotten water, said take
the curve of a daffodil

bending toward snow, but leave the field.

They took nothing, left a memory of river, wild raspberry, and honey.

the light gentles the daffodil upward

honours daffodils broken from the stem, daffodils frozen before
flowering, daffodils stepped on, driven over, eaten, ignored

honours days without light, ground without water, plants that flower
too early and those that flower too late, bulbs that never sprout

and light at different angles touching other grounds.

the optic nerve the light excites

Incident rays strike our eyes

Rods and cones convert incidence to signal

From the retina's cells to the millions of cells in each optic nerve to the optic chiasm to the brain

The signals cross in the optic nerves' crossing

Crossing the optic nerves the signals enter the brain

The image a minor unpredictable accompaniment

Whether the fern is blue or green

the light uninterpretable

A moonless night.
A strange mountain lightness at the top of the hill.
There is more sky here between two valleys than any other place.
It has a strange effect with the dark at night.
Seems a kind of light.

one hill at a time, the light moves in strides, covering

My presence can add nothing

My disappearance take nothing away

strike a light

a. Wrestle from field a skin of sun.

b. Pollen lined lines lining you.

c. Undoubt the weather.

d. Grow sky from seed and eat it.

e. Nothing retaliates.

f. Beekeepers burn empty hives in the street.

the lighthouse revolving

Yesterday, late afternoon light fell at an angle incoherent
with my thought, and I knew nothing well. This morning
there was little light and knowing seemed silly, the decadence
of dismissible chance. Now, I know enough to feel that sensing
the mind's dissolution and calling it perception is possibly
dangerous. Requires a body and mind and soul and voice
and pollen and vegetative density that have the freedom
to dissolve. To become what is glimpsed from the corner
of an eye. However briefly. Or a felt absence. In lightning
flashes to escape the laws of the world, these flashes lightening
us.

Notes

"If light stabilizing / If to receive a bee," which begins on page 27, is indebted to Londa Schiebinger's *Plants and Empire: Colonial Bioprospecting in the Atlantic World.*

Pg. 58 after Jean-Jacques Rousseau

The "sea blooms and oozy woods" on page 75 are Percy Bysshe Shelley's.

Pg. 99 after Lady Mary Wroth

Pg. 109 after Dorothy Wordsworth

Acknowledgements

An earlier versions of "Once Sun" appeared in *The Malahat Review.* Thank you to the editors for that publication.

To Jay MillAr and Hazel Millar, thank you for this book and for the process by which it came to be.

My profound gratitude for you whose kindnesses have helped shape this work:

Elizabeth Acorn, Tassie Adamson, Cara Benson, Caetlin Benson-Allott, Kyle Chocorlan, Helen Berggruen, Ava Dellaira, Kate Desormeau, Sarah Ensor, Anne-Lise François, Peter Gizzi, Louise Glück, Claire Hansen, Soula Harisiadis, Elizabeth Harvey, Ruby Knaffo, Nate Link, Sarah McNeil, Audrey Medina, Doug Paisley, Mia Pancaldo, Victor Platt, Hilary Rand, Joseph Ronsenberg, Anita Sokolsky, Sam Sokolsky-Tifft, Yasmin Solemnescu, Anthony Stark, Anna Swann-Pye, Steve Tifft, Walter and Marcia Unger and the Unger family, Cheryl Ward, Anna Weber-Kneitel, Opal Vandeloo, and Julia Zarankin.

An especial thank you to Cate Williamson and Dorothy Wang and to Mark, Linda, Amanda and Annie.

Gratitude that lacks the power to conclude to Richard Carpenter, Karen Swann, Jane Gregory, and Sarah Weiger, to my parents, John and Maria Joosten, my brother, Michael Joosten, and to Zoe Unger, always and again, it is the better with me . . .

About the Author

Julie Joosten grew up in Marietta, Georgia. She has an MFA from the Iowa Wrters' Workshop and a PhD from Cornell University. She lives in Toronto. *Light Light* is her first book.

Colophon

Manufactured as the First Edition of *Light Light* in the Fall
of 2013 by BookThug. Distributed in Canada by the Literary
Press Group: www.lpg.ca. Distributed in the United States
by Small Press Distribution: www.spdbooks.org. Shop on-
line at www.bookthug.ca

BOOK
PRODUCTION
WAR ECONOMY
STANDARD

Text + design by Jay MillAr
Copy edited by Ruth Zuchter